Taking Action

TAKING ACTION AGAINST
Eating Disorders and Body Image

Caroline Warbrick

rosen publishing's
rosen central

New York

Published in 2010 by The Rosen Publishing Group Inc.
29 East 21st Street, New York, NY 10010

First Edition

Editor: Camilla Lloyd
Consultant: Jayne Wright
Designer: Tim Mayer
Picture researcher: Kathy Lockley
Artwork: Ian Thompson

Library of Congress Cataloging-in-Publication Data

Warbrick, Caroline, 1961-
  Taking action against eating disorders / Caroline Warbrick.
    p. cm. – (Taking action)
  Includes index.
  ISBN 978-1-4358-5344-7 (library binding)
  ISBN 978-1-4358-5472-7 (paperback)
  ISBN 978-1-4358-5473-4 (6-pack)
  1. Eating disorders–Juvenile literature. I. Title.
  RC552.E18W375 2010

616.85'26–dc22

2008053336

Picture acknowledgments: The author and publisher would like to thank
the following for allowing their pictures to be reproduced in this
publication: Cover photograph: Don Smetzer/Stone/Getty Images. ACE
STOCK LIMITED/Alamy: 17T; Angela Hampton Picture Library/Alamy: 32;
Bubbles Photolibrary/Alamy: 6, 19, 21T, 25, 35T, 42; Charles
Gullung/zefa/Corbis: 43; Corbis: 44; David J. Green - Lifestyle/Alamy: 8T;
Don Hammond/Design Pictures/Corbis: 14; Don Smetzer/Stone/ Getty
Images: 18; Emely/zefa/Corbis: 37; Goodshoot/Corbis: 30-31;
Greg Ceo/Jupiter Images: 9; Heiko Wolfraum/dpa/Corbis: 7; Karl Prouse/
Catwalking/Getty Images: 29; Kazuyoshi Nomachi/Corbis: 27; Lori
Adamski Peek/Stone/Getty Images: 38; LWA-Dann Tardiff/Corbis: 15,
34B; Nicoloso/ photocuisine: 3 bkg., 4T bkg., 5B bkg., 8B bkg., 10T bkg.,
16T bkg., 17B bkg., 21B bkg., 23, 26T bkg., 28T bkg., 34T bkg., 35B bkg.,
39 bkg., 40-41T bkg., 46-47T bkg., 48 bkg.; North Wind Picture Archives/
Alamy: 10CR; P.M.Images/Getty Images: 45; Profimedia International
s.r.o./Alamy: 28B; Randy Faris/Corbis: 12-13; Rick Gomez/Corbis: 40B;
Roger Bamber/Alamy: 26B; SGO/Image Point FR/Corbis: 5T; Steve
Skjold/Alamy: 16CL; Trustees of Watts Gallery, Compton, Surrey/
Bridgeman Art Library: 11; Ute Klaphake/ Photofusion Picture Library: 1,
22; Wayland Archive: 47; Will & Deni McIntyre/Corbis: 4B, 33; Zave
Smith/Corbis: 20; Zigy Kaluzny/Stone/Getty Images: 41.

Manufactured in China

CONTENTS

Chapter 1

What are eating disorders?

We all have different eating habits and enjoy a wide variety of foods. Just think about you and your friends. What are your favorite foods? How much do you like to eat? If you ask people, it's very likely that you'll find a great deal of difference in how and what people eat. With such variety, it's really difficult to know what is a normal eating style. Yet the term *eating disorder* implies that there are some ways of eating that are a problem.

What does it mean to have an eating disorder?

Eating disorder is the name given to problems relating to a person's eating style. There are three main ways in which people can have difficulties with their eating. These are when they eat too little, when they eat too much, or when they do harmful things to themselves to get rid of the food they have eaten.

There are so many different eating styles that it can be difficult to decide what is normal and what isn't.

Eating disorders are not just about how someone eats but about how they think and feel about themselves and food.

However, eating disorders are not just about how someone eats. They also related to how people think and feel about themselves, their bodies, and food. People with eating disorders are often very unhappy, and the way they cope with this unhappiness is through their eating. When trying to decide whether or not someone has an eating disorder, doctors don't just look at how a person eats. They also look at a person's body to find out whether they have the physical symptoms of an eating disorder, and they examine how they behave and how they think and feel, particularly about themselves and about food.

Eating disorders are some of the most difficult illnesses to understand and diagnose. In order to decide whether someone is at risk of developing an eating disorder or already has a problem, doctors need to have a clear idea of what an eating disorder is, and what the symptoms are. In the next few chapters, we will see what types of eating disorders there are, what puts someone at risk of developing an eating disorder, and what we can do to help ourselves and others.

FACTS

* ✳ Eating disorders are not just about food but are a sign of unhappiness.
* ✳ The body, behavior, the thoughts, and the feelings of a person are affected when someone has an eating disorder.
* ✳ The people most likely to be affected by an eating disorder are young women and girls between the ages of 15 and 25.
* ✳ Between 1% and 5% of young women are affected by anorexia.
* ✳ Eating disorders include anorexia nervosa, bulimia nervosa, and compulsive eating disorder.

Types of eating disorders

There are a number of ways in which people's eating can be disordered, but the most serious eating disorders are anorexia nervosa, bulimia nervosa, and compulsive eating disorder (also know as binge eating disorder).

Anorexia

People with anorexia (anorexics) are obsessed with being thin and do what they can to avoid putting on weight. The behavior of anorexics is often characterized by excessive dieting and exercising and very controlled eating habits. Anorexics are often extremely thin, yet they still see and describe themselves as overweight.

Bulimia

Bulimics (people with bulimia nervosa) are also concerned with being thin. However, they are also greatly troubled by food and eating. People with bulimia are often caught in a cycle of uncontrollable eating, called binging, followed by periods of purging. *Purging* is the name given to the strategies that bulimics use to get rid of the food they have eaten. Bulimics are also troubled by obsessive thoughts. When they are not eating, they are thinking about food. When they have binged, they feel terrible about themselves and their behavior and are driven to get rid of the food they have consumed.

People with eating disorders look in the mirror and hate what they see. They often think they are bigger than they really are.

Sometimes people try to control their weight by vomiting after meals.

Compulsive eating disorder

People with compulsive eating disorder also find it hard to stop eating or thinking about food. However, unlike bulimics, they do not purge. Consequently, many people with this form of eating disorder are overweight. Many obese people are deeply unhappy about the way they look. They don't want to be fat, but they find losing weight difficult.

It happened to me

"When I look back, I think the signs were all there, it's just that we never suspected that she had a problem. She'd never buy anything to eat at breaktime or have lunch with us. She used to make excuses that she had to go to the library or something. When she did hang around with us, she seemed really distant. Then she started to lose weight. I remember her getting changed for gym and thinking that her arms and legs were just skin and bones, and that she might snap at any time. Then one day, she didn't come to school. The teachers said she was very sick and needed to be at home."

Many young people are concerned about how they look. Their insecurities are not helped by being confronted with "perfect" images of models in magazines.

The difficulties in diagnosing eating disorders

It is very difficult to decide whether or not someone has an eating disorder. This is because many of the behaviors and feelings that people with eating disorders have are present to some degree in most of us. For example, how many people do you know who are on a diet, or who worry about their weight or how much they eat? How many of your friends are unhappy with the way they look and think they are bigger than they really are?

FACTS

* It is estimated that two out of five women and one in three men are unhappy with their body, particularly their weight.

* Two out of three people are currently on a diet.

* Weight is the most disliked aspect of the body.

* By the age of ten, most girls are afraid of becoming fat.

* Most women who are a normal size also overestimate their body size—not just anorexics, as formerly believed.

* The demand for cosmetic surgery is rising, particularly among young women. The most common procedures undertaken are breast augmentation (changing the size and shape of breasts), nose jobs, and anti-ageing procedures.

Behavior

At the present time, at least 60 percent of us claim to be on a diet. Yet, at the same time as many of us are trying to lose weight, concerns about overeating and being overweight are growing. One question facing doctors is when does dieting, or overeating, become a problem and an indication of an eating disorder? What is too little or too much?

Thinking and feeling

Low self-esteem and unhappiness with the body are key features of eating disorders. Yet these thoughts and feelings are not just experienced by people with eating disorders. Many of us admit to being very dissatisfied with how we look. Research shows that nearly half of women and a third of men are unhappy with the way they look, and issues of weight are the things they are most unhappy about.

People want to look good. Often teenagers with eating disorders look in the mirror and dislike what they see.

Chapter 2

Food and the body

Although eating disorders appear to be a modern day problem, our relationship with food and eating has been complicated for a long time.

Feasting and fasting

During the Roman Empire, the rich became experts in overeating and it was normal to vomit after enjoying a large meal. From the Middle Ages, saintly people were famous for their prolonged periods of fasting. Fasting was believed to bring a person closer to God. In the 1300s, St. Catherine of Siena was famous for her ability to live on very small amounts of food. It was said that she would take a twig and stick it down her throat to make herself vomit!

The emergence of anorexia

Although cases of people fasting have been reported over the centuries, it was not until the nineteenth century that anorexia nervosa became a recognized illness and the "fasting girl" became a serious problem for Victorian doctors. It is also around this time that we start to see a range of food-related illnesses appearing. One explanation for the emergence of anorexia in Victorian society was that refusing food was one way in which woman could express their unhappiness. In the Victorian era, food was one of the few areas in life where women had some control.

Food has always played an important role in our social life and celebrations. The picture above shows a Roman feast.

In Victorian England, if women were frail and slim, they were considered to be feminine and attractive.

There also appeared to be a link between the way "ladies" were expected to behave and how they managed their eating. To be frail, pale, and thin was fashionable for middle-class Victorian women. Eating tiny amounts became associated with femininity and overeating became associated with anything that was distasteful. Appetite was associated with ugliness, indulgence, and lack of control.

TALK ABOUT

By studying eating disorders throughout history and in society today, we can see that some messages sent out about food, eating, and the body may have played a role in the increase in eating problems and disorders.

✳ Why do you think women in particular have been more prone to suffering from problems with their eating?

✳ Do you think it is important for a woman to be slim? If so, why?

For ideas on how to extend Talk About discussions, please see the Notes for Teachers on page 47.

Food, bodies, and society

It can seem as though some parts of Western society, especially the media, are sending out a number of contradictory messages about food, eating, and the body. On one hand, food is used to celebrate many of the festivals and events in our lives, and eating together is an important social activity. We also live in a society that persuades us to eat for all kinds of reasons other than to satisfy our hunger. On the other hand, although we are encouraged to eat more, we are also told that eating too much, eating the wrong foods, and being fat and unfit are bad.

Sociable eating

Sharing food is not only an important and enjoyable way of spending time with others, it is also an area where we might be expected to show restraint and manners. Overeating and indulgence are sometimes frowned upon, and those who overeat are seen as greedy and lazy. Such contradictory messages seem to have an impact on us all and feed into the complex relationship many of us have with food and eating.

It happened to me

"Food is so complicated . . . I don't know how to feel about it. I have a mother who comments on my appearance and weight, but then cooks me delicious food and expects me to eat all of it. If I don't, then she gets upset. It's as if her giving me food is a way of showing she cares. I know I am not as slim as I would like to be, but how do I lose weight when life in my family revolves around meals and food?"

Sharing food is an important social activity in many cultures.

In our society, being slim, especially for women, can be seen by some as a part of being attractive. We are bombarded daily with images of celebrities looking attractive and thin. The impression we're given is that they naturally look this way and have thrown together their image effortlessly. In reality, the media often presents a slimmer than average woman as an ideal, and the pictures of the celebrities have been airbrushed to get rid of imperfections. Even celebrities sometimes express surprise at the images they see of themselves in magazines! Often, those who rely on their looks for a living spend many hours each day at the gym, the beautician's, or hairdresser's, keeping their looks in tip-top condition. Many models are on permanent diets to keep their weight down and complain about the pressures to look good all the time.

Prejudice

We are bombarded with misleading media images that have an impact on many of us. We feel that in order to be attractive, we have to look like these "ideals." This can lead to us having difficulties in accepting, or being happy with who we are.

In our relationships, too, we communicate views about being fat or eating too much. These views can be very powerful. We often tease one another about being fat, and being teased about weight is a common experience for many young people. But teasing can have a devastating effect, and as a result, many young people start dieting and may develop eating disorders. Larger people are often the butt of jokes and are criticized for being unhealthy, lazy, and greedy. They find it hard to buy fashionable clothes that fit, and are sometimes criticized and misunderstood by doctors who tell them that they must lose weight. Many people who are overweight speak of being overlooked in job interviews or of finding it hard to make friends or attract a partner.

Pictures of beautiful and thin models like the one below reinforce the idea that image is important.

Society

For many people, it can be a struggle to maintain a body weight appropriate to their height and build. This is particularly difficult in a society where commercials encourage people to eat more and more. These people are also faced with society's general prejudice against overweight people. This just makes matters worse.

Try putting together a collage of pictures and articles from the media that are concerned with body image. For example, find some stories about your favorite celebrity and articles about clothes or makeup. Think about what message is being communicated to you by all these stories and pictures.

The media is a powerful force in promoting ideas about body image and what is attractive.

TALK ABOUT

Look at these statements about the role of the media in the increase in eating disorders. Do you agree or disagree with them?

✳ Slim bodies and perfect figures are more valued than other qualities by the media and by society.

✳ The messages we get from the media play a massive role in the development of eating disorders.

✳ Eating disorders could be caused by lots of factors and aren't caused by the portrayal of the ideal figure in the media at all.

Chapter 3

What does it mean to have an eating disorder?

Eating disorders are not just about food, they are a sign of unhappiness.

As we have seen, concerns about the body and problems with eating are present in many people. So how are eating disorders different from the day-to-day concerns about weight, body image, and dieting that many of us experience?

Unhappiness

First, it's important to remember that eating disorders are not just about problems in eating, but are a sign that someone is deeply unhappy. Their problems with eating are a result of this unhappiness. People with eating disorders do have problems with food, but they also have problems with how they think and feel. So when doctors have to decide whether someone has an eating disorder, they look for a number of signs in the thoughts, emotions, and behavior of a person and try to assess how much of a problem these are. Some of these signs are easy to recognize; they include the physical symptoms that directly result from eating disorders. Other signs are harder to detect; they include the way a person feels and thinks about themselves and their behavior toward food. It is relatively easy to tell when someone has extreme problems. But it is much more difficult to make judgements about thoughts, emotions, and behavior that are only slightly different from usual.

Young people with eating disorders often feel as though they don't fit in as part of the group.

FACTS

When diagnosing an eating disorder, doctors look for a number of signs (known as symptoms). Eating disorders have symptoms that affect:

* The body.
* Behavior.
* Feelings.
* Thoughts.

Signs of an eating disorder

There are three main types of eating disorder: anorexia nervosa, bulimia, and compulsive eating disorder. With each of these, there are physical symptoms and changes in the feelings, thoughts, and behavior of the person that suggest that they might have a problem with eating.

Anorexia nervosa

Anorexia nervosa means "loss of appetite for nervous reason." However, this definition is slightly misleading, because the person has not lost their appetite. In fact, anorexics often feel very hungry, they just don't allow themselves to satisfy their hunger.

Anorexics expend a lot of energy on avoiding food, but anorexia is not really about food at all. The roots of anorexia lie in unhappiness and low self-esteem. Such feelings have led the anorexic to develop a set of strategies that help them feel better about themselves. Eating very little, or being extremely thin, appears to bring a sense of achievement and pride, which boosts self-esteem.

Even when they are very thin, anorexics constantly see themselves as overweight.

The physical symptoms of anorexia are mostly the result of not eating enough. People who have anorexia are underweight for their age and height. They are sick more often than normal, and may complain of feeling dizzy, cold, and weak. In young women, a key sign of anorexia is the loss of menstrual periods.

It happened to me

"Dieting has always been a huge part of my life. I was feeling fat by the time I was 11. When I was 12 years old, my mother paid me $20 to lose 10 pounds. I was overweight but not too much. It made me feel gross. Everyone seemed to be saying, when you're thin, you're prettier, you'll get boyfriends, people will like you. My sisters were pretty, thin, and good at everything—school, sports, boys. I was the chubby little sister. Then I found dieting and I could be perfect at that. I could go all day on water, a slice of tomato, and a slice of pepper. By the time I was 14, I weighed just 84 pounds . . . It wasn't until recently when I looked through some old pictures that I realized I was never fat!"

Thoughts and behavior

Many anorexics think about themselves in distinctive ways. They usually have a distorted view of their body—seeing themselves as fat even when they are really very thin. Anorexics also experience a range of emotions. Depression, anxiety, unhappiness, disgust, and guilt are common feelings for anorexics.

Often people with anorexia behave strangely, especially in relation to food. They seem to possess an enormous willpower and are able to resist food for long periods of time. Many anorexics appear to be obsessed by food and are anxious to cook and prepare it for other people. However, they are unwilling to eat themselves. When they do eat, they have strange rituals, such as chewing each piece of food many times or cutting it up into very small pieces.

People with eating disorders often behave strangely at mealtimes. They sometimes push food around their plates to make it appear as though they have eaten some of it.

Bulimia

Bulimics also have problems with their eating and weight. However, rather than starving themselves, bulimics regularly and often secretly eat large quantities of food and then attempt to control their weight by vomiting, crash dieting, or using laxatives.

Typically, a bulimic episode begins with a session of binge eating where large amounts of food are eaten. During a binge, bulimics often describe feeling out of control and unable to stop eating. Following a binge, the bulimic feels disgusting and guilty. In order to relieve these feelings, they then attempt to get rid of the food they have eaten by making themselves sick or by taking laxatives (purging). Some bulimics also try to balance what they have eaten by exercising excessively.

Bulimia is very distressing. People with anorexia or bulimia can become obsessed by thoughts of food and eating.

Purging

Purging means that the person quickly becomes hungry again. The hunger is accompanied by obsessional thoughts about eating. These thoughts are hard to get rid of. The cycle of binging and purging is repeated again and again and is difficult to break.

Bulimia is much harder to detect than anorexia, since bulimics are often of normal weight and take great care to hide their sickness. However, there are signs that suggest someone may be suffering from this disorder. If someone has been bulimic for a while, there will be physical changes to the body. Regular vomiting can lead to a sore throat, tooth and gum decay, and poor skin. Binge eating can cause the stomach to become bloated and painful, and regular use of laxatives can lead to constipation.

A bulimic episode typically starts with a period of binge eating.

FACTS

* Bulimia affects between 1% and 2% of young women.

* It is thought that more people suffer from compulsive eating disorder than from anorexia and bulimia. However, people are less likely to seek help for it.

* Although girls are ten times more likely to suffer from anorexia and bulimia than boys, eating disorders are becoming more common in young men.

The causes of bulimia

As with anorexia, the causes of bulimia lie in the way people feel about themselves. Their attitude to food is a symptom of a deeper problem and unhappiness.

Signs of bulimia also show up in the way someone thinks and feels. Bulimics find it difficult to stop thinking about food. They also have a distorted view about how they look and are often desperately unhappy. People with bulimia behave in odd ways, particularly around food. A common sign of bulimia is when a person disappears to the bathroom soon after eating.

After eating, bulimics feel disgusted with themselves and are driven to rid themselves of the food they have just eaten.

Often during a binge, large amounts of cakes, cookies, chocolate, and candy are eaten.

It happened to me

"I would start to think about food as soon as I got up. I would go to the supermarket and buy ice cream and a couple of packs of fudge-brownie mix. On the way home, there was a bakery. I'd stop, buy a dozen doughnuts, and start eating them even before I was walking out the door. When I got home, I'd mix the brownies and put them in the oven. Then, while they were baking, I would eat the ice cream. When the brownies were ready, I would start to eat them, even if they were still hot. Although I would only intend to eat two or three, pretty soon I would have eaten almost all of them. I'd try to stop by throwing them in the garbage, but I'd just get them out again. Then the guilt hit. I'd go to the bathroom and make myself throw up. I was so good at it that it was almost automatic—just instant vomiting, over and over, until there was nothing coming out of my stomach."

Compulsive eating disorder

Compulsive eating disorder (also known as binge eating disorder) shares many common features with bulimia. In both disorders, overeating is central and the person feels guilt and remorse over their eating. However, the main way in which compulsive eaters differ is that after a binging session, they do not try to rid themselves of the food they have consumed. As a result, many compulsive eaters are overweight.

People with compulsive eating disorder behave in distinct ways. When eating a meal, they often consume large quantities of food and eat more rapidly than others. They also eat large amounts of food when they are not hungry. They do this by continuously eating (grazing) or binging on large amounts of food in one session.

Typically, the compulsive eater is always on a diet. They often try really hard to lose weight and control their eating. However, very often their efforts are undone by a small lapse, which then turns into a full-blown binge. For example, a compulsive eater might say "I've blown it, so I might as well forget my diet until tomorrow..." They often make themselves unrealistic promises such as, "I will only be good if I can lose some weight." People with this disorder feel unhappy about their eating and say they hate themselves and the way that they look.

TALK ABOUT

Should we worry about children's weight and what they eat? Look at the following statements. Do you agree or disagree with them?

* Childhood eating habits can determine adult food tastes and the body's metabolic rate; so obese children are more likely to become obese adults.

* Obese children are storing up health problems for later on in life.

* Many children will lose their excess weight as they grow up.

* Obsessing over a child's eating habits or size makes them unhappy and can even lead to more problems with eating.

For many people with compulsive eating disorder, food is a source of comfort. Often the person feels sad or lonely, and they eat to make themselves feel better.

Compulsive eating, like anorexia and bulimia, is an ineffective way of dealing with stress or with deep-rooted unhappiness, loneliness, or low confidence. Overeating carries health risks. Most significantly, many binge eaters are overweight, and in a growing number of cases, obese. Most doctors treat obesity as a serious health risk. Obese people are roughly twice as likely to need hospital treatment and are more likely to suffer from high blood pressure, heart disease, strokes, and diabetes than people of a healthy weight.

Chapter 4

Who gets eating disorders?

Anyone can develop an eating disorder. However, the people most likely to be affected are young women between the ages of 15 and 25. Anorexia typically begins at, or just after puberty, and bulimia occurs in slightly older young women, around 18. More people suffer from compulsive eating disorder than from anorexia and bulimia. Again, although both men and women are affected by it, it is more common in women and more women seek help for it.

Risk factors

There are a number of factors that increase the likelihood that someone will develop an eating disorder. They include personality, past experience, and society. It has also been found that certain professions have higher than average rates of eating disorders. These include dancing, modeling, and horse racing. In all these professions, the pressure to maintain a slim body appears to make the person more vulnerable.

Eating disorders have been found to be more common in professions where there is a pressure to be thin.

Gender

Although eating disorders are more common in women, over the past few years, there has been a rise in the number of reported cases of eating disorders in men. Men involved in sports professions appear to be at particular risk. This is because they place a lot of importance on weight and physique. Recently, a new condition has been identified—exercise anorexia. This illness appears to be much more common in men than women. A combination of excessive exercising and dieting characterizes the condition exercise anorexia. The person affected is obsessed with being at a peak level of fitness.

Research shows that eating disorders are more common in models and dancers.

One concern of those who work with eating disorders is that men, young men in particular, are not getting the help they need. This is because young men are reluctant to seek help when they are suffering from eating disorders. They feel ashamed, because eating disorders are seen as a female problem.

It happened to me

Simon is a champion jockey and has recently admitted to a long battle with anorexia nervosa. Simon admitted that his desire to succeed as a jockey led him to suffer from the eating disorder from the age of 16. Simon says, *"Concern with my weight became an obsession. The less I ate the less I wanted to eat. Basically, I had starved myself to be a jockey . . . "*

Chapter 5

What causes eating disorders?

It is unlikely that an eating disorder results from a single cause. It is much more likely that a combination of factors contributes to the development of these disorders. Researchers believe that a number of risk factors make it more likely for someone to develop an eating disorder.

Social pressures and the media

Females are far more likely to develop eating disorders than males. It appears that the society in which we live puts immense pressure on women to be slim and this can have an effect on the development of problems with eating.

Females are more likely to develop eating disorders.

Our social surroundings have a powerful influence on our behavior. Societies that don't value thinness have fewer eating disorders. Body image and slimness are seen to be important in Western culture (culture that is typical of North America and western Europe). We are judged on our appearance and are often encouraged to improve ourselves. The media sends out strong messages about what we should look like. Many of us are affected by these messages and try to achieve the ideals we are shown. However, for most of us, these ideals are unrealistic. One common feature of people with eating disorders is that they feel very unhappy about themselves and who they are. One way they think they will feel better is by becoming thin.

Fashion

The fashion industry is being urged by some to ban the use of "size 0" models. (Size 0 relates to a women's clothing size in the U.S.—it is the equivalent of a U.K. 4 or a European 32–34.) Size 0 is sometimes used to describe people with a Body Mass Index (BMI) below 18.5. People with such low BMIs are usually very underweight. The model population is seen to be at significant risk of developing anorexia or bulimia, and it is estimated that 20–40 percent of models suffer from some sort of eating disorder. However, despite these concerns, super-skinny models continue to be used throughout the fashion industry.

The fashion industry is thought to play a role in the development of eating disorders as it can be seen to glamorize thinness.

In the media

Recently, a model died during a fashion week in Uraguay. The model's family claimed that she had fasted for days after being told by her modeling agency that she could make it big as a model if she lost weight. Her death, and worries about the health of skinny models, led to a ban on size 0 models in the Madrid fashion shows. It was expected that the shows for London Fashion Week in the U.K. would also ban size 0 models from the catwalks. However, this did not happen, and many people in the fashion industry spoke out about the backlash against size 0 models. One designer argued, *"The British Fashion Week should not comment or interfere in the aesthetic [look] of any design show."* Another claimed, *"Just because a girl is skinny, it doesn't mean she is unhealthy."*

Personality

Some research suggests that certain personality types are more likely to suffer from eating disorders. For example, people with a tendency to perfectionism are thought to be more vulnerable to anorexia. A need for control also appears to be a feature of eating disorders. It can be very satisfying to diet. Most of us know the feeling of achievement when the scales tell us that we have lost a couple of pounds. It is good to feel that we can control ourselves in a clear, visible way. It may be that, with eating disorders, weight is the only part of life over which someone feels they have any control.

Most people with eating disorders have low self-esteem. People with low self-esteem don't think much of themselves and compare themselves unfavorably to other people. Losing weight and being thin can be one way of trying to improve self-esteem. However, self-esteem cannot be permanently raised by dieting or weight loss. In order to really feel better about themselves, people have to learn to accept and love themselves for who they are.

Family life

Eating is an important part of family life. Making food for others to eat gives pleasure to the cook. It can be upsetting if someone refuses to eat the food we cook.

Families also play a crucial role in the development of a child's self-esteem. Children who are raised in homes where they are constantly criticized, rejected, or given little love and encouragement may grow up feeling unlovable or unworthy. Many people who have eating disorders have low self-esteem.

Family quarrels and stress can trigger eating disorders. Sometimes saying "no" to food is the only way that a child can express him or herself and have a say in family affairs.

TALK ABOUT

Look at what you have learned about eating disorders.

✱ What do you think is the main cause of people's dissatisfaction with their bodies?

✱ What do you think about the use of size zero models on the catwalks?

✱ Do the media and the fashion industry contribute to problems of body image? Are they to blame?

Emotional distress

Difficult challenges have also been found to trigger eating disorders. We all react differently when bad things happen or when our lives change. Eating disorders are clearly related to a variety of problems that people have experienced. These problems include stress, such as taking exams, difficult family relationships, and upsetting events, such as the death of a loved one.

Adolescence

Although there appears to be a range of factors that contribute to the development of eating disorders, one factor seems to be common to most. Eating disorders almost always begin in adolescence, and most people with eating disorders claim that they started to have problems in their teenage years.

There seems to be a number of things about becoming and being a teenager that can contribute to eating problems. When a young person becomes a teenager, he or she has to cope with a lot of changes. These include coming to terms with puberty and being expected to behave more like an adult. Young people also start to think about their identity a lot more, and there might be pressures on them to look good and fit in. It is in adolescence that people seem to be particularly affected by the pressures to look slim and attractive.

Eating disorders often begin in adolescence. Many young people feel under enormous pressure to look good, and this can lead to problems with body image and eating.

Eating disorders tend to be more common in young people who are high achievers and want to do well.

TALK ABOUT

What do you think are the challenges of adolescence? Think about the different things young people are expected to achieve at this age, for example, starting high school and getting a boyfriend or girlfriend.

✳ What difficulties do you think teenagers face in trying to adapt to these changes and expectations?

✳ Why do you think that adolescence is sometimes associated with the development of a number of problem behaviors such as eating disorders?

Chapter 6

Preventing problems

After reading this book, you may feel that you have an eating disorder, or the early signs of one. If you have any suspicions, then it's really important to act on them. It's much easier to prevent eating disorders in their early stages, and there are a number of things you can do to help yourself.

Helping yourself and others

It's really important that you don't bottle things up. Find someone you can talk to, for example, a teacher, relative, or doctor, and tell them how you are feeling, that you are worried about yourself and think you may have a problem. If they just say "don't worry," then confide in someone else who will take you seriously.

If you are worried about yourself, it is important to find someone you can talk to.

A doctor, teacher, or school nurse can help you find the support and advice you need.

Besides talking about how you are feeling, you can also ask for help in finding out more about eating disorders. There is a list of organizations and helplines on page 47, which you might find useful. You can also try your local surgery, library or Connexions service. It is always useful to find out as much as you can about eating disorders, their symptoms and treatment. By doing so, you can define the problems you might have and find out what you can expect from treatment. It will also help you to realize that you are not alone. This in itself can be very comforting.

FACTS

If a doctor thinks a person has an eating disorder, he or she may ask the questions below. If the patient answers "yes" to two or more of these questions, then they may have an eating disorder.

✳ **Do you make yourself sick after eating?**

✳ **Do you worry that you've lost control over how much you have eaten?**

✳ **Have you recently lost more than 13 pounds (6 kilograms) in three months?**

✳ **Do you believe that you're fat when others say that you're thin?**

✳ **Would you say that food dominates your life?**

Improve your self-esteem

Poor self-image can be at the root of many eating disorders, so improving your self-esteem can be one way of helping yourself. There are a number of things you can do to feel better.

Try to accept yourself for who you are. Next time you are with other people, take a look around. You will see that people come in many different shapes and sizes. There is no such thing as "normal," and the images you see in the media don't reflect the way most of us look. Instead of thinking about what you're not, think about what you are! What do you like about yourself? Don't just focus on your body, think about your personality, your talents, and your interests. What are you proud of? What do people like about you? Think about the people you like. Do you like them because they are thin or because they are fun, creative, or caring? We are all born different, so feel good about, and make the most of, your individuality.

This diagram shows the different food groups that make up a person's diet. The key to a healthy diet is to eat a wide variety of foods, including fruit and vegetables, and not to eat too much fat or sugar.

Eat healthily

The diagram on the right gives you an idea of what you should try to eat each day. You should eat starchy foods (the biggest section) with every meal. You should have at least two portions of protein, such as nuts, eggs, fish, and meat. Dairy products, such as milk and cheese, are good for our bones and teeth because they contain calcium. You should aim for at least one portion of a dairy product every day. A healthy diet consists of eating lots of fruit and vegetables and only a small amount of sugary foods and drinks.

Asking for help

Remember that your body will change in adolescence and it might need to settle down before you think about going on a diet. If you think that you need to lose weight, then perhaps you could visit your doctor or school nurse. They will tell you whether you are the right weight for your height and body type. If you are not, they can give you advice on how to eat healthily. Learning to eat properly can be good for you in lots of ways. It will help you achieve a weight that is right for your height and body shape, and it will ensure that you eat the right foods. This then will have a positive effect on your mind and body.

Eating fruit or other healthy snacks and drinking lots of water can help you improve your diet.

Exercise regularly

Exercise is a great way of toning your body and will also make you feel good in the process. There are lots of ways to exercise. Walk to and from school instead of getting the bus; take the stairs rather than the elevator. Go swimming, rollerblading, or trampolining. As you start to feel more confident, you should aim to build three 20-minute sessions of some form of exercise into your week.

Controlling what you eat

If you are troubled by binging, there are a number of things you can do to help yourself control what you eat. Think about when you are most likely to binge and try to find ways of avoiding these danger times. For example, avoid situations where you might eat or buy food out of habit. If you always buy candy or doughnuts on the way home, then go a different way. Put snack foods in places where it is difficult to reach them. Ask whoever shops for you to avoid buying the foods you are most likely to binge on. If you're more likely to binge when you are bored, then try to keep yourself busy and occupied at danger times.

There are lots of fun ways to exercise and keep fit.

DOs & DON'Ts

* Eat regular meals—missing meals encourages overeating.

* Eat a balanced diet—one that contains all the types of food your body needs.

* Take regular exercise.

* Think about your good points.

* Try not to be influenced by other people skipping meals or commenting on weight.

* Don't weigh yourself more than once a week.

* Don't spend time checking your body and looking at yourself in the mirror. Nobody is perfect. The longer you look at yourself, the more likely you are to find something you don't like.

* Don't look at websites that encourage you to lose weight and stay at a very low body weight. They encourage you to damage your health, but they won't do anything to help you when you are really sick.

Chapter 7

The treatment of eating disorders

It is usually very difficult for people with a serious eating disorder to get better on their own and most will need some help. There are many people that can help with eating disorders, including doctors, counselors, dieticians, and psychologists. The treatment offered will depend on the type of eating disorder, how serious it is, and its causes.

The treatment of eating disorders focuses on the whole person and aims to help the sufferer to feel better about themselves.

Help

Most people with eating disorders receive help while they go on with their daily lives. However, in severe cases, the sufferer may have to spend some time in the hospital or in a specialist eating disorder clinic. Most treatments try to work on the whole problem and use a combination of strategies that aim to improve eating habits, as well as help the sufferer feel better about themselves.

In the early stages of treatment, the sufferer may receive advice about healthy eating and may talk with a counselor to try to find out about why the illness has developed. Sometimes the sufferer will be encouraged to join a support group. Here, they can meet with other people with eating disorders to talk about their condition and find ways to support each other on the road to recovery. The aim of treatment is not just to get the person to eat healthily, but to help them feel better about themselves.

Hospital

If the person needing help is in danger of becoming very sick, they will be admitted to the hospital. There, the first goal will be to stabilize their eating and help them gain weight, so that they are within the healthy range. One way to help a person with anorexia is through a treatment that gives them rewards for eating and putting on weight. Such rewards might include trips out and having personal possessions in the hospital. The person will also meet with a therapist or counselor, to start to explore their eating problems and find ways of overcoming them and feeling happier in themselves.

Support groups where people with eating disorders can share their experiences can be an important source of help and advice.

It happened to me

"I was admitted to an eating disorders clinic when my weight dropped to 84 pounds. The first goal was to get me to eat and put on weight. When I started eating, then I was allowed to have some of my own things back and small treats, like my choice of food. After I started putting on weight, I was allowed to visit home. My goal is to reach my target weight and go home."

What we can do to help others?

When a young person asks for help for an eating disorder, there are a number of things that friends and family can do to support them. First, it is useful to learn about eating disorders and their treatment. This will enable you to understand some of what they might be going through and help you to support them through the process. You might feel that you are not doing very much to help, that you are just listening and being supportive. Don't undervalue what you are doing. Just being there for someone is a very important job.

Just listening to someone talk about their worries about body image is important and can help them.

If you live with someone who has an eating disorder, try to make your home supportive. Remove scales, diet books, and calorie counters and be sensitive to the kind of food you keep around. Keeping large amounts of cake, chips, and cookies, particularly in very obvious places, may not be helpful. However, don't banish all food and eating in the presence of the person with the eating disorder. You need to try to strike a balance and be relaxed in your attitude toward food.

It is important to make meal times as stress-free as possible when you are eating a meal with someone who has an eating disorder.

Mealtimes

If you're eating with someone who suffers from an eating disorder, then try to make mealtimes as relaxed as possible. Don't police how much they eat or try to encourage them to eat more. Think carefully about how you socialize with people who are being treated for eating disorders. For example, going out for a pizza or hamburger might become a stressful experience for a bulimic or an anorexic.

In the media

The Internet has enabled a number of specialist websites to spring up. "Pro-anorexia" sites are an example of such sites. These sites are run by anorexics to celebrate and promote anorexia. Such sites give advice on how to lose weight and show pictures of emaciated people. They also offer the opportunity for anorexics to discuss their condition and strategies for losing weight. A number of groups, including doctors, parents, and teachers, are concerned about such websites, their easy availability, and their lack of regulation, and fear that they are playing a part in the rise of eating disorders. There have been articles in the press about the danger of these websites.

Personal attitudes

It's also important for all of us to think about the way we describe and talk about people. Don't make comments about your own weight or that of anyone else, particularly critical comments. People with eating disorders are likely to be very sensitive to any comments about their appearance, and even a positive comment on their weight can be devastating. Some anorexics thrive on being told they look terrible or are much too skinny.

Society

Finally, think about the environment in which you live. Are you reinforcing the slim ideal by the posters you put up and the magazines you buy? Even if it is only on a small scale, we all need to think about the things we do in relation to our bodies and weight. For example, at school, ask for books and magazines that reflect the way we really look. Celebrate individuality, difference, and diversity—and remember beauty comes from within!

We need to accept ourselves and others for who we are and not for what we look like.

You can find useful advice on the Internet about eating disorders and how to get help.

Information and advice

There are a number of organizations that offer support and advice for those wanting to find out more about eating disorders. Most of them can send free information packs and leaflets. Some will offer to answer questions over the phone or by email. These organizations may also be able to provide you with details of regional groups and associations in your area. Useful organizations and websites are listed on page 47.

TALK ABOUT

✱ **What do you think about websites that promote eating disorders?**

✱ **Do you think that there should be more control over the Internet and websites such as these?**

Glossary

anorexia or anorexia nervosa A lack of appetite for food. An emotional disorder involving an obsessive desire to lose weight by refusing to eat.

binging Eating large amounts of food.

body image The way someone sees their body.

bulimia or bulimia nervosa An emotional disorder involving overeating, usually alternating with fasting or self-induced vomiting or purging.

calorie A unit for measuring the energy value of food.

compulsive Overwhelming urge to do something.

constipation Difficulty in going to the toilet.

dehydration Lacking water or fluid in your body, which causes many side effects.

depression Severe unhappiness, especially when long-lasting.

diagnose To recognize a disease through its signs and symptoms.

eating disorder Medical condition in which people either undereat (anorexia) or overeat (compulsive eating disorder) or deliberately vomit (bulimia).

emaciated Very thin.

fasting Deliberately going without food.

hormones Chemical substances in the body that perform important functions.

laxatives Pills that stop you from digesting food by making you go to the toilet.

metabolic rate The rate at which your body uses up calories.

obese Weighing more than 20 percent above normal requirements for height and body shape.

obsession Thought that won't go away and seems uncontrollable.

psychological Relating to the mind and behavior.

psychologist Someone who has trained to work with and understand people with problems.

purging Getting rid of food that has been eaten or digested by vomiting or taking laxatives.

risk factor A condition or factor that increases the likelihood of something happening.

rituals Behaviors that are carried out in regular, routine ways—such as always preparing food in the same way or eating it in the same order.

therapy A method of understanding and solving problems by talking, guided by a trained specialist.

Further information and Web Sites

Notes for Teachers:

The Talk About panels are to be used to encourage debate and avoid the polarization of views. One way of doing this is to use "continuum lines." Think of a number of opinions or statements about the topics that can be considered by pupils. An imaginary line is constructed, which pupils can stand along to show what they feel in response to each statement (please see above). If they strongly agree or disagree with the viewpoint, they can stand by the signs; if the response is somewhere in between, they stand along the line in the relevant place. If the response is "neither agree, nor disagree" or they "don't know," then they stand at an equal distance from each sign, in the middle. Continuum lines can also be drawn on paper and pupils can mark a cross on the line to reflect their views.

Books to read

Anorexia Nervosa: A Survival Guide for Families, Friends and Sufferers
Janet Treasure
(Psychology Press, 1997)

Bulimia Nervosa and Binge Eating: A Guide to Recovery
Peter Cooper
(NYU Press, 1995)

The Eating Disorders Update: Understanding Bulimia, Anorexia and Binge Eating
Alvin Silverstein
(Enslow Publishers, 2008)

Unlocking the Mysteries of Eating Disorders
David B Herzog
(McGraw-Hill, 2007)

Web Sites

Due to the changing nature of Internet links, Rosen Publishing has developed an online list of Web sites related to the subject of this book. This site is regularly updated. Please use this link to access this list:
http://www.rosenlinks.com/act/eati

Index

Entries in **bold** are for pictures.